THE ABCs OF ATX

WRITTEN BY KELLY SHARP

ILLUSTRATED BY JOY BURAN + NOELLE MELODY

Printed in Canada

Fourth Printing, 2019

ISBN: 978-0-692-52093-2

Triple Dog Press
www.TripleDogPress.com

FOR VICTOR

TO ALL TINY AUSTINITES LEARNING THEIR LETTERS,
HERE'S HOPING THIS BOOK MAKES THE PROCESS MUCH BETTER.

6

AND TO AUSTINITE PARENTS, READING ALOUD,
HERE'S HOPING THIS BOOK DOES OUR LITTLE TOWN PROUD.

A

IS FOR AUSTIN, OUR CAPITAL CITY,

WE RATHER LIKE IT, FOR IT'S RATHER PRETTY.

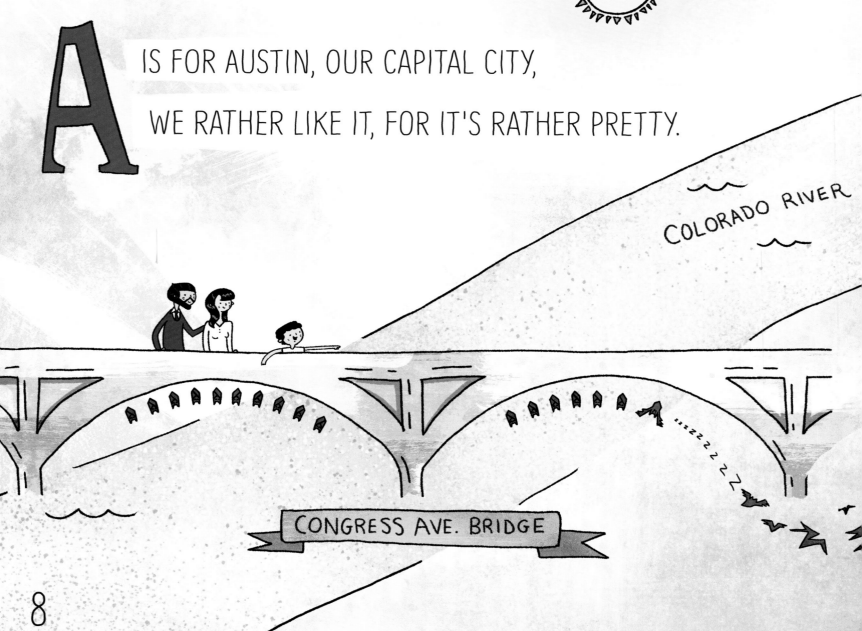

COLORADO RIVER

CONGRESS AVE. BRIDGE

8

B FOR OUR BATS,

WHO SLEEP UPSIDE DOWN,

WAKE UP AT SUNSET,

AND HEAD INTO TOWN.

9

C IS FOR CONGRESS, FIRST AMONG STREETS—

10

COME FOR THE CAPITOL, STAY FOR THE TREATS.

11

BIG  FOR DALLAS, THAT METROPLEX WHERE

THE BUILDINGS ARE ALMOST AS **BIG** AS THE HAIR.

13

E IS FOR EEYORE, WHOSE BIRTHDAY EACH YEAR

F IS FOR "FIXIN'," USED IN PLACE OF "ABOUT TO."

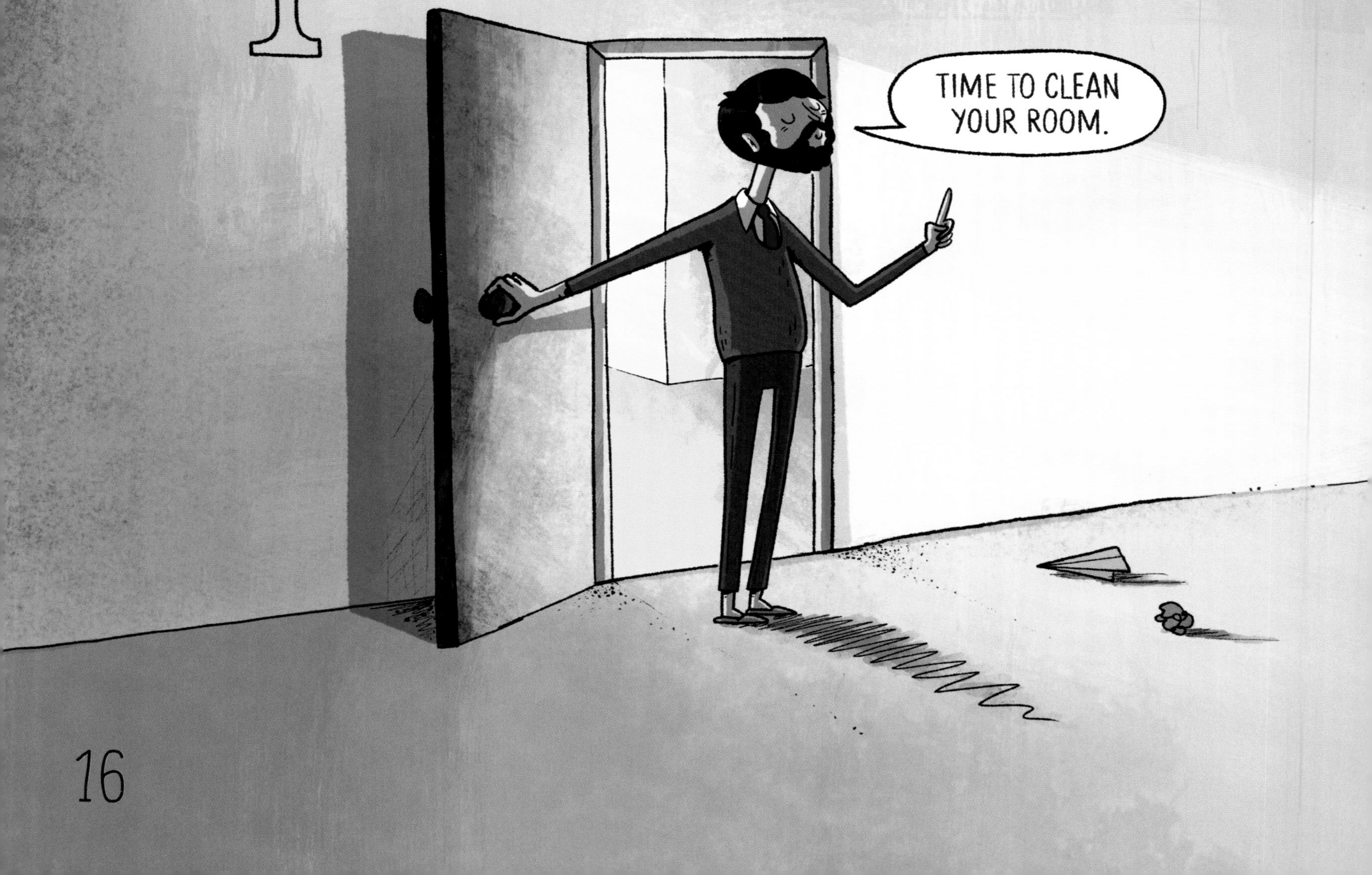

ALSO, IN MANCHACA, WE DON'T SAY THE LAST "A"—
IT'S EASY TO SPOT OUT-OF-TOWNERS THIS WAY.

I IS FOR ICY,

THAT BARTON SPRINGS FEEL—

22

ONCE YOU'VE LIVED HERE
IN SUMMER,

YOU'LL SEE THE APPEAL.

23

J'S JALAPEÑO, THAT HOT LITTLE CHILI—
EATING TWO IN ONE BITE WOULD BE TERRIBLY SILLY.

THAT WAS TERRIBLY SILLY.

K IS FOR KUT & KUTX

...WITH YOUR HAPPY FEET DANCE PARTY COMING UP NEXT!

L IS FOR THE LADY BIRD WILDFLOWER CENTER—

ALWAYS IN BLOOM, EVEN IN WINTER.

N

FOR NOSTALGIA, REMEMBERING HOW

AUSTIN USED TO BE COOLER THAN IT IS, SOMEHOW, NOW.

P

IS FOR THE HALLOWED TRADITION OF POTLUCKS—

IS FOR QUESO,

THAT MAGICAL DIP

36

THAT, PAIRED WITH SALSA,

TRANSFORMS EVERY CHIP

TO A Velvety Dream

FROM A LONESOME CORN SLIP.

R IS FOR ROACHES,

THE SIZE OF SMALL DOGS,

38

EASILY SQUISHED WITH A
PAIR OF OLD CLOGS.

 **S** IS FOR SWIMMING,

AND SUMMER,

AND SUN!

40

WHEN THE TEMPERATURE HERE IS A HUNDRED AND ONE.

41

WHICH YOU WON'T HARDLY NOTICE IF YOU DON'T HARDLY DRIVE.

W

WILL WALTZ ACROSS TEXAS WITH YOU
AT THE WHITE HORSE, THE BROKEN SPOKE, AND THE RATTLE INN, TOO.

X IS IN TEXAS, OUR GIANT HOME STATE,
WE KNOW IT'S NOT PERFECT, BUT ISN'T IT GREAT?

Y IS FOR "Y'ALL"

A MOST EXQUISITE CONTRACTION.

48

USE IT TO CALL TWO OR MORE FOLKS TO ACTION.

GIVES WAY TO SPRINGTIME AND THE TAILS OF KITES.

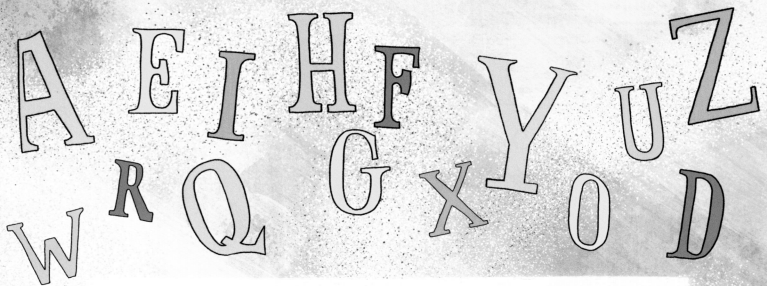

NOW YOU KNOW AUSTIN, AND YOUR ABCs, TOO.
GO FORTH! GO EXPLORE! THERE'S SO MUCH TO DO!

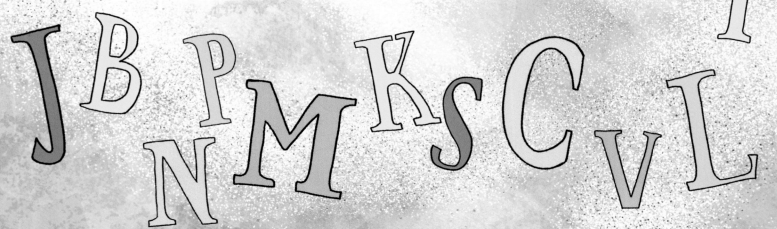

AND WHEN YOU GROW UP (AND MAYBE GROW YOUR OWN BEARD!), WE'LL NEED ALL OF YOUR HELP TO KEEP AUSTIN WEIRD.

THE END

KELLY

KELLY SHARP GREW UP IN TEXAS, ATTENDED SOUTHWESTERN UNIVERSITY, AND CALLS AUSTIN HOME. SHE WROTE HER FIRST ABCs BOOK WHEN SHE WAS 3 YEARS OLD, WITH SUBSTANTIAL HELP FROM HER MOTHER. NOW, SHE WRITES SHORT FILMS, SHORT STORIES, AND OTHER FUN PROJECTS. IF THERE'S A MORE PERFECT FOOD THAN TACOS, SHE HASN'T FOUND IT YET.

YOU CAN FIND HER HERE: WWW.TRIPLEDOGPRESS.COM

JOY + NOELLE

JOY BURAN & NOELLE MELODY ARE ILLUSTRATORS, ANIMATORS, AND, AS IT HAPPENS, TWINS. THEY BOTH EARNED BFAs IN MEDIA ART FROM PRATT INSTITUTE IN BROOKLYN; THEIR THESIS FILM WAS THEIR FIRST COLLABORATION. SINCE THEN, THEY'VE MADE SHORT FILMS, COMMERCIAL ANIMATIONS, CHILDREN'S BOOKS, AND DECOUPAGE GLASS ART. JOY LIVES IN QUEENS AND NOELLE LIVES IN KINGSTON, NY; THEY KEEP A ROOM IN EACH OTHER'S HOUSE AND A NOOK IN EACH OTHER'S BRAIN. EACH ALSO KEEPS AN EXQUISITE COLLECTION OF CHARMING OBJECTS AND CHARMING PETS, FROM WHICH THEY DRAW INSPIRATION. BRING THEM COFFEE, OR ELSE.

YOU CAN FIND THE TWINS HERE: WWW.JOYANDNOELLE.COM